EDGE BOOKS™

THE KIDS' GUIDE TO

PROJECTS
FOR YOUR PET

by Gail Green

CAPSTONE PRESS
a capstone imprint

Edge Books are published by Capstone Press,
1710 Roe Crest Drive, North Mankato, Minnesota 56003.
www.capstonepub.com

 Books published by Capstone Press are manufactured with paper
containing at least 10 percent post-consumer waste.

Library of Congress Cataloging-in-Publication Data
Green, Gail.
The kids' guide to projects for your pet / by Gail Green.
    p. cm.—(Edge Books. Kids' guides)
Includes bibliographical references and index.
Summary: "Step-by-step instructions show how to make simple projects for
    pets"—Provided by publisher.
ISBN 978-1-4296-7662-5 (library binding)
1. Pets—Miscellanea—Juvenile literature. 2. Handicraft—Juvenile literature.
    I. Title.
SF416.2.G75 2012
745.592—dc23   2011029261

Editorial Credits
Carrie Braulick Sheely, editor; Kyle Grenz and Tracy Davies McCabe, designers;
    Wanda Winch, media researcher; Marcy Morin, project production; Sarah
    Schuette, photo stylist; Eric Manske, production specialist

Photo Credits
All images Capstone Studio: Karon Dubke, except: Dreamstime: Michael
Pettigrew, cover (cat and dog); Shutterstock: Eric Isselée, cover (parrot),
back cover

Printed in the United States of America in Stevens Point, Wisconsin.
032013   007240R

TABLE of CONTENTS

INTRODUCTION

Chances are that you and your pet share a bond unlike any other. Creating something for your pet can be a great way to show how much you care about it. You get to use your creativity, and your pet gets to enjoy the finished project. All you need is your imagination and a few supplies, including items you may already have around the house.

Before You Begin

Before you begin, gather a few general supplies. You'll use these in at least one of the projects.

- ruler
- yardstick
- tape measure
- pencil
- scrap paper
- sharp-tipped scissors
- non-toxic craft tacky glue

- masking tape
- 2-in (5-cm) wide painting sponges or paint brushes
- large paper plate or large shallow container that can be discarded after use
- rags or paper towels

Sewing Know-How

A few projects include sewing. Take a minute to review some sewing basics to make sure your stitches will stand up to even the rowdiest pet.

Choosing a needle: The holes in needles are called eyes. Eye sizes vary depending on the type of needle. Use a general purpose needle called a sharp when hand sewing with thread. When using embroidery floss or yarn, use a needle with a larger eye, such as a chenille or embroidery needle.

Thread the Needle and Knot the Thread:
Cut 12 to 18 in (30 to 46 cm) of thread. Insert the thread into the eye and pull the thread through. Keep pulling the thread until about 4 in (10 cm) of thread is on one side of the needle. This will be the "tail." Wrap the long end of thread twice around your index finger. Hold the thread between your thumb and index finger. Roll the thread away from and off your index finger. The threads should twist together. Once the thread is off your finger, hold the loop and pull it down to form a knot.

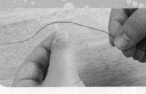

hand stitching: As you hand stitch, try to keep your stitches the same length and keep them spaced evenly.

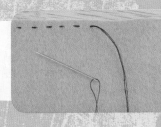

overcast stitch: Overcast stitches loop around a fabric's edge. They should be **parallel** and uniform in length. Beginning on the fabric's **wrong side**, push the needle up through the fabric. Bring the needle around the edge of the fabric and back to the wrong side. Insert the needle about 0.25 in (0.6 cm) from the first stitch. Continue until you have completed your row of stitches.

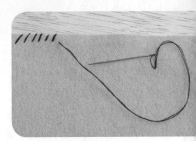

finishing knot: You must secure your thread when it is not long enough to continue stitching or when you have reached the end of a row of stitching. Make sure you have 4 to 5 in (10 to 13 cm) of thread left. Make two or three small stitches on the wrong side of the fabric next to the last stitch you made. Insert the needle through and out of one of the stitches. Repeat and tighten to form a knot. Trim leftover thread.

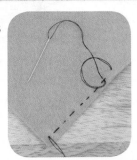

parallel—an equal distance apart

wrong side—the back side of fabric; the wrong side often does not have colors and textures like the right side does

TREAT CONTAINER

Fill this colorful treat container with yummy treats for your special pal. You can even teach your pet good manners by asking it to sit and wait before receiving the treat.

1. Measure the height of your oatmeal container and add 1 in (2.5 cm). Measure around the outside of your container.

2. Using these measurements, cut a rectangle from black craft foam.

TIP:

INSTEAD OF CRAFT FOAM, YOU CAN USE FELT, FABRIC, PRINTED CARDSTOCK, WRAPPING PAPER, OR GROCERY BAGS.

3. Place the oatmeal container on a scrap or a second sheet of black craft foam. Trace two circles around the base and cut them out. Glue to top and bottom of container.

diameter—the length of a straight line through the center of a circle

4. Place your mug on the yellow craft foam sheet. Trace around it with your pencil. Repeat on the remaining sheets until you have traced 10 circles in at least three different colors.

5. Cut out all the circles and place them on your table. Use the fabric paint to draw curved lines on each of the circles. You can use a tennis ball for reference. Let the paint dry completely, following instructions on paint bottle.

6. Place the circles as desired on the craft foam rectangle and glue them on.

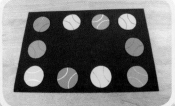

7. Use the fabric paint to write your pet's name or other words of your choice in spaces between the circles. Let dry.

8. Apply glue to both the container and the back of the craft foam rectangle. Carefully wrap craft foam around the container and press in place until the glue holds the foam. Trim to fit when dry.

LOVE THAT LIVER TREATS

Some of the treats you eat may not be good for your pet because they include things like sugar and salt. But these liver treats are **nutritious** for your cat or dog, and your pet will love the taste!

1. Preheat oven to 350ºF (180ºC).

2. Ask an adult to help you cut the raw liver into 2-in (5-cm) chunks. Place the chunks in a blender or food processor.

3. Add the water and run the blender or food processor on the chop setting until smooth.

What You Need

knife and cutting board

blender or food processor

medium-sized mixing bowl

spoon

9- by 13-in (23- by 33-cm) metal or glass baking pan

spatula

1 pound (455 g) beef or chicken livers

½ cup (120 mL) water

2 eggs

1 teaspoon (5 mL) garlic powder

1 tablespoon (15 mL) dried or 3 tablespoons (45 mL) fresh chopped parsley

½ teaspoon (2.5 mL) dried or 1 tsp (5 mL) fresh chopped basil

2 ½ cups (600 mL) whole wheat flour

1 cup (240 mL) corn meal

cooking oil, shortening, or non-stick cooking spray

nutritious—containing elements the body uses to stay strong and healthy

4. Pour the liver into a medium-sized bowl. Add the remaining ingredients.

5. Mix well with a spoon.

6. Grease the pan with oil, shortening, or non-stick spray. Pour the mixture into the pan and spread evenly with spatula.

7. Bake in the oven for 25 to 30 minutes until dry but not crispy.

8. Let cool for 20 minutes. Cut into 0.5-in (1.3-cm) cubes. Keep treats refrigerated for up to three days or frozen for up to two months.

TIP:

TO CHECK IF YOUR TREATS ARE DONE, STICK A TOOTHPICK IN THE CENTER AND PULL IT OUT. IF THE MIXTURE STICKS TO THE TOOTHPICK, COOK FOR ANOTHER 5 MINUTES. TREATS ARE DONE WHEN THE MIXTURE NO LONGER STICKS TO THE TOOTHPICK.

DECOUPAGE PET ENVIRONMENT

Lizards, frogs, turtles, hermit crabs, snakes, and other animals that live in tanks or habitats are happiest when they feel safe and secure. Decorate your pet's tank or habitat with a **collage** that looks like its natural environment.

What You Need

nature images from used greeting cards, wrapping paper, printed scrapbook paper, printed cardstock, or other **porous** paper materials

tissue paper in assorted colors

newspaper

nontoxic decoupage paste

waterproof non-toxic varnish or decoupage sealant

BEFORE YOU BEGIN:

- The collage can be created on one to four sides of a tank. The number of sides you decorate will depend on the **opacity** of the images being glued onto the tank or habitat and your individual pet's needs.

- Most pets need some light. Avoid completely covering the glass or plastic with images. If you prefer to cover the sides more completely, create your collage with tissue paper. This type of paper is translucent and allows more light to pass through.

- This project must be created and completely dry before placing your pet inside.

- Decorate only on the outside of the tank or habitat.

- Do not use stickers or other images that are self-adhesive.

- Do not use images printed on coated stock. This paper has a smooth glossy finish. Ask a store clerk if you're unsure if the paper is coated or uncoated.

collage—an arrangement made by gluing different items onto a flat surface

porous—allowing liquid to soak through

opacity—how see-through a material is

1. Cut or hand tear images from paper, greeting cards, cardstock, etc. Cut leaf, flower, and other shapes from tissue paper.

2. Lay newspaper on your work space to protect it. Arrange the cut-out shapes and images until you are happy with the design.

3. Beginning at the bottom of the tank, apply decoupage paste in a thin layer to a small section.

4. Work with one piece of paper at a time. Apply decoupage paste to the front and back of each piece to soak it completely. Place images on tank. Add thin layers of paste over all the images so the pieces stick smoothly onto the tank. Work quickly in small sections. The key to preventing bubbles and getting images to stick is to keep everything wet.

5. Continue adding pieces and paste until the scene is complete. Let dry several hours or overnight.

6. When completely dry, brush on two coats of waterproof varnish or sealant. Let dry completely per instructions on container.

GO FISH CAT TOY

Your cat will have hours of fun playing with this soft toy fish. After it's done, you can use your sewing skills to create even more toys for your feline friend.

1. Create a pattern by drawing an oval fish body shape about 3.75 in (9.5 cm) wide and 4.5 in (11.5 cm) tall on scrap paper and cutting it out. Place the pattern on two layers of felt. Trace around the shape and cut it out. Be sure to cut through both layers of felt.

2. Cut strips of felt in the following sizes. Use one color for the fins and another for the tail.
- top fin—2 strips measuring 2 by 2 in (5 by 5 cm) each
- bottom fin—2 strips measuring 2 by 1.25 in (5 by 3.2 cm) each
- tail—6 strips measuring 1 by 4 in (2.5 by 10 cm) each

3. Cut six 1.5-in (3.8-cm) long fringes along each top fin and three 1.5-in long fringes along each bottom fin. Cut two 3.5-in (8.9-cm) fringes on each tail strip. Be sure to leave a 0.5-in (1.3-cm) **seam** allowance on each fin and tail strip.

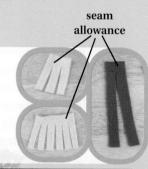

seam allowance

seam—a line of sewing that joins two pieces of material

4. Create eyes by cutting two pieces of felt 0.5 in (1.3 cm) in diameter. Use a color different from the body pieces.

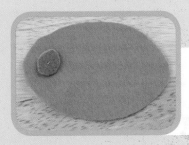

5. Make three stitches through the center of each eye to attach them to the **right side** of each fish body.

6. Place fish body pieces wrong sides together. Place the fin and tail pieces slightly into the fish body. Pin in place.

7. Using an overcast stitch, sew around the fish body. Sew through all layers (including fins and tail pieces where appropriate). Leave a small hole at the front so you can stuff the fish with scraps of felt or catnip. Sew shut after stuffing.

Overcast Stitch
see page 5

TIP:

DECORATE THE FISH BODY BY SEWING ON STRIPS OF CONTRASTING COLORED FELT OR FLEECE BEFORE STITCHING TOGETHER.

right side—the front side of fabric

FRAID-E-BRAIDS

Do you enjoy playing with your dog? Soft but strong, this colorful tug toy is specially designed so you and your dog can play with it together.

1. Cut out 15 fleece strips and place in a stack, alternating colors as desired.

Use this guide
for sizing the strips:

- **Cut 1.5- by 34-in (3.8- by 86-cm) strips for a small dog.**
- **Cut 2- by 40-in (5- by 102-cm) strips for a medium-sized dog.**
- **Cut 2.5- by 44-in (6.4- by 112-cm) strips for a large dog.**

2. Tie all the strips together in the center with a single knot.

TIP:

YOU CAN MAKE A LARGER KNOT BY INCREASING THE NUMBER OF STRIPS AND MAKING THEM WIDER.

3. Braid strips together to create 5 braids on each side of the knot. Tie a single knot at the end of each braid.

4. Create eyes by cutting out two white felt circles 1 in (2.5 cm) in diameter and two black circles 0.5 in (1.3 cm) in diameter. Place each black circle on top of a white circle.

5. Sew eyes onto the knotted ball. Insert needle into the center of one eye through both felt layers and into the knotted ball. Pull the needle out of ball ⅛ in (0.3 cm) from the first hole and insert the needle back through the felt eye. Repeat four to six times. Cut off excess thread.

SAFETY NOTE: Only give this toy to pets that are not aggressive chewers. Pets should be supervised during play, and the toy should be checked regularly for wear. If your pet starts to chew or eat parts of this toy, remove it or replace the toy.

15

DOG T-SHIRT

Turn your dog into a canine fashionista with this T-shirt using handmade stamps and stencils. You may even want to create a matching shirt for yourself!

MAKE YOUR STENCILS:

1. Tear off several 10- to 12-in (25- to 30-cm) long pieces of wax paper. Draw 2- to 3-in (5- to 8-cm) wide shapes of your choice on the wax paper. Draw only one shape in the center of each piece. Some shape suggestions are hearts, stars, and bones.

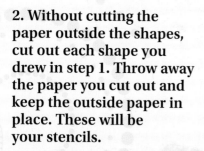

2. Without cutting the paper outside the shapes, cut out each shape you drew in step 1. Throw away the paper you cut out and keep the outside paper in place. These will be your stencils.

TIP:

THIS PROJECT CAN BE VERY MESSY! PROTECT YOUR TABLE AND WEAR OLD CLOTHES THAT CAN GET PAINT ON THEM.

MAKE YOUR STAMPS:

1. Remove one protective sheet from the adhesive and attach to the back of the craft foam sheet. Draw or trace paw print or other shapes on the foam using a pen or stylus.

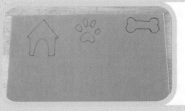

2. Cut out the shapes, remove the protective paper, and attach them to the scrap wood.

PROJECT INSTRUCTIONS:

1. Try the T-shirt on your dog to make sure it fits. The T-shirt should be loose around the neck but fit tightly around your dog's stomach. Cut the neck hole wider if necessary. Remove the T-shirt.

2. Slip the T-shirt over the cardboard. Fold the sleeves around the back of the cardboard and tape them. The cardboard will keep the paint from seeping from the front of the shirt to the back.

3. Squeeze a blob of brush-on paint about the size of a quarter onto a paper plate. Spread it out with a cosmetic wedge. Press your stamp into the paint, remove it, and stamp on the T-shirt. Repeat these steps using stamp images and colors of your choice. Let dry completely.

continue on next page

4. Place a stencil on the T-shirt, overlapping stamped images if desired. Tape in place around stencil edge. Spray paint per manufacturer's instructions in center of stencil. Carefully blot off excess paint from stencil and remove. Let dry.

5. Repeat step 4 until you are happy with your design. Let dry completely.

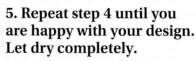

6. Write your pet's name and fun phrases on the T-shirt using the dimensional paint. Add dots, squiggles, and other decorations if desired.

TUBES AND TUNNELS FUNHOUSE

Your hamster or gerbil will love exploring the bends and turns of this rodent playground. It even has skylights and tubular bling! You'll have hours of fun watching your pet play.

What You Need

four clean, empty cardboard facial tissue boxes with all plastic removed

four cardboard toilet paper, wrapping paper, paper towel, or shipping tubes sized appropriately for your pet to climb through (The tubes should not have glue residue on them.)

construction paper, paper bags, art paper, or unused paper coffee filters (All paper must be nontoxic.)

single-hole paper punch

MAKING THE FUNHOUSE

1. Place a tube 1 to 2 in (2.5 to 5 cm) above the bottom of a tissue box on the short end. Trace around the tube end. Carefully cut out the circle, and insert the tube 1 in (2.5 cm) into the box. Cut another circle on the long end of the box that is farthest away from your first cut-out.

2. Repeat drawing and cutting out circles on all four boxes. Complete your structure by inserting the tubes and connecting the boxes to form a square. Use the punch to add small air holes every 6 in (15 cm) in tubes longer than 8 in (20 cm).

continue on next page

MAKE TUBE CHAINS

1. Depending on the diameter of your tubes, cut 18 to 24 paper strips for each chain. The paper strips should measure 1.5 by 4.25 in (3.8 by 10.8 cm).

2. Fold each strip as follows: Fold both long edges together. Open. Fold each long edge to line up and meet along the middle fold. Repeat first fold. Fold both short edges together. Open. Fold each short edge to line up and meet along the middle fold to form two looped tabs.

3. Insert strips into each other by placing folded tabs into the tabs of the next strip.

4. Wrap each chain around a tube. Tuck each end between the tube and box to secure.

SAFETY NOTES:
- Your pet must be supervised at all times when playing in the funhouse.
- Use boxes and tubes that do not contain adhesive, stickers, or ink in areas where your pet can chew.
- Exit tubes should be inserted no higher than 1 in (2.5 cm) above the bottom of a box.
- Replace soiled tubes and boxes as needed.

MAKE THE SKYLIGHTS

1. For each skylight, cut two paper rectangles 1 in (2.5 cm) larger than your tissue box on all sides.

2. Cut several long 0.5-in (1.3-in) wide strips from one rectangle. Set aside.

3. Measure and cut parallel slits 0.5 in (1.3 cm) apart and 1 in (2.5 cm) in from each side of the second rectangle. Cut and remove every other strip.

5. Place each skylight above an open box top.

4. Loosely weave strips from step 2 through the slits.

DENIM SLEEPING MAT

Show your pet how much you care with a cozy place to nap! This project is also a great way to recycle worn or outgrown clothing.

What You Need

pair of new or used jeans in a size appropriate for your pet

needle and thread

thimble

pen

large metal eyelets

eyelet setting tool with anvil

small tack or craft hammer

soft washable items (small blankets or throws, towels, T-shirts, sweatshirts, etc.)

roll of 0.25- to 0.5-in (0.6- to 1.3-cm) wide fabric ribbon

1. Lay jeans flat on your work space. Cut along both inside seams of jean legs.

2. Sew inseams together so fabric lays flat. If needed, use a thimble to help you push the needle through the fabric.

TIP:

MAKE SURE THE JEANS HAVE NO RIPS, HOLES, OR SLASHES. AVOID CHOOSING JEANS WITH PAINTED OR GLUED-ON OBJECTS.

3. Starting at the bottom hem of the jeans, measure and mark eyelet holes every 1.5 in (3.8 cm) with a pen. Mark along the entire bottom hem. Do the same at the waistband of the jeans.

4. Trace the inside of an eyelet over each mark. Carefully cut out each hole with scissors. Do the same at the waistband of the jeans.

5. Follow the directions on the eyelet packaging for setting the eyelets at the bottom hem and waistband.

6. Insert soft washable items inside the jeans as desired.

7. Cut two pieces of ribbon 24 in (61 cm) long each. Starting at one end of the bottom hem, thread the ribbon through the eyelets. Come up through the back eyelet, into the front eyelet, and then over the hem. Then bring your ribbon through the next back eyelet. Continue doing this until you have threaded your ribbon through all the eyelets. Repeat this step at the waistband.

8. Cut two more pieces of ribbon 24 in long. Thread this ribbon through the eyelets the opposite way as in step 7 so the ribbons cross.

9. Tie the ribbons in a bow at each end of the eyelet rows. Be sure the waistband is shut.

TIP:

MAKE A TOY FOR YOUR PET AND INSERT IT INTO ONE OF THE POCKETS IN THE MAT.

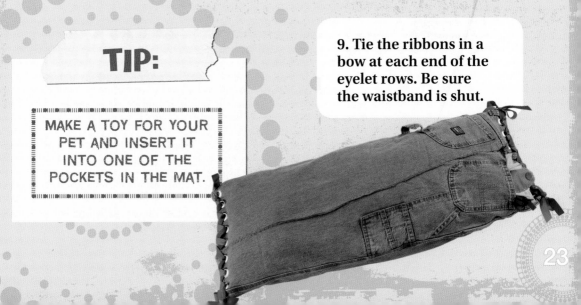

23

SLIP-ON COLLAR DECORATION

Jazz up your pet's collar for everyday use or for special occasions. You may even want to make different versions for every holiday!

What You Need

two pieces of felt or fleece, each a different color (Use pattern instructions below to determine size.) These pieces will be sewn to slip over the collar.

straight pins

embroidery thread in assorted colors

embroidery needle

12-in (30.5-cm) felt squares in assorted colors

fabric or tacky craft glue

assorted beads or gems

MEASURE AND MAKE THE PATTERN

1. Place your pet's open collar on the table. Measure the widest (A) and thickest (B) parts of the collar. (The widest and thickest parts may be a double thickness, a buckle, loop, or choke chain ring. Do not measure the ID tag loop.) You must also include an additional 0.5 in (1.3 cm) for seam allowance (C). Add A, B, and C together to get your pattern width (PW).

2. Measure the length of the collar when on your pet's neck. (Do not include snap-on buckles or choke chain rings). Divide that measurement by .75 to get your pattern length (PL).

3. Draw a pattern on scrap paper that measures PL x PW. Cut out the pattern. Draw 0.25-in (0.6-cm) seam lines along the long edges.

PROJECT INSTRUCTIONS

1. Place the pieces of felt with contrasting colors together. Position the pattern on top, pin it in place through all layers and cut out. Remove pins and pattern.

2. Pin felt layers together. Using embroidery thread, make overcast stitches along the long edges through both layers. Stitch through each individual layer along the short edges so the felt collar decoration is open at each end. Make sure the stitches are within 0.25 in (0.6 cm) from the edge. Try to make your stitches all the same length.

Overcast Stitch
see page 5

3. Draw and cut out small felt shapes (bones, hearts, stars, etc.) from the 12-in (30.5-cm) felt squares. Glue onto the collar decoration. Glue beads and gems on as desired. Let dry before slipping onto your pet's collar.

TIP:

GLUE ON SILK FLOWERS OR A FANCY BOW TO MAKE YOUR COLLAR DECORATION STAND OUT.

25

NO-SEW CAGE AND CRATE COVER

Everyone needs a little privacy at times—including pets that live in cages or crates. Your cage cover could even match your room or living area.

What You Need

- fleece (Use instructions below to determine size.)
- large sheets of paper (blank newsprint, scrap paper, or paper grocery bags)
- straight pins
- large fabric cutting board with measurement grid printed on it (optional)

FIND YOUR DIMENSIONS:

This project will cover five sides of your cage: the top, front, back, and two sides. Since cages are not standard sizes, each cage will have different dimensions.

TIP:

THE TW AND SW DIMENSIONS SHOULD BE THE SAME!

How Many Yards of Fleece Will You Need?

Here's the Formula:
- Measure the top of your cage from front to back for depth (TD). Measure the cage from side to side for width (TW).
- Measure the sides of your cage from top to bottom for height (SH) and from side to side for width (SW).
- Add SH + TW + SH + 12 in (30.5 cm). This is dimension A. Add SW + TD + SW + 12 in (30.5 cm). This is dimension B.

CREATE YOUR PATTERN:

1. Using a pencil, draw and cut out one top piece from the paper: TW x TD.

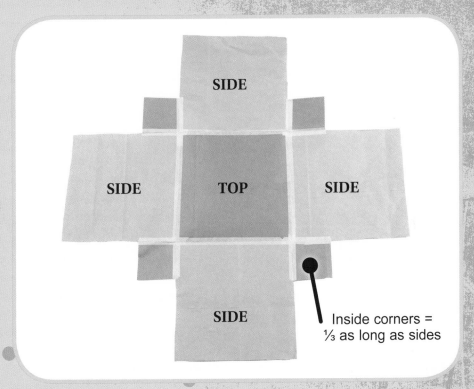

SIDE

SIDE   TOP   SIDE

SIDE

Inside corners = ⅓ as long as sides

2. Draw and cut out four side pieces:

SW x SH + 6 in (15 cm).

Label each piece. Tape four side pieces to the top piece.

3. Draw and cut out four inside corner pieces to allow for the extra corner material you'll need. Make these corners one-third as long as the sides. Tape these pieces to your pattern.

continue on next page

PROJECT INSTRUCTIONS:

1. Make sure your table surface is protected. Then place two layers of fleece with right sides together on the table. Place pattern piece on the fleece and pin in place. Cut around pattern.

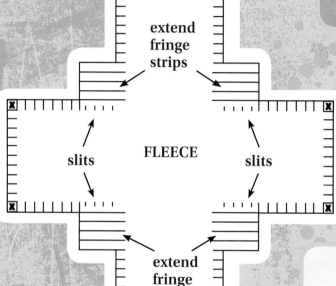

extend fringe strips

slits

FLEECE

slits

extend fringe strips

LEGEND:
X = cut out pieces
—— = fringe strips

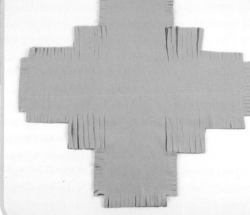

2. Cutting through both layers, cut 1-in (2.5-cm) wide fringe strips along all four sides as shown. Also cut out pieces in corners as shown in above diagram. The corner cut-outs should be the same length as the fringes on both sides.

3. Tie both layers of each fringe strip together in a single knot. Extend the fringes on the inside corners until they meet with the ends of the strips on the rest of the fleece. Don't tie the inside corner fringes yet.

4. Mark and cut 0.75-in (1.9-cm) long slits through both layers of fleece along the inside corners of your cage cover. Slip two fleece strips through the double layer slits on opposing sides. Tie together in a single knot as before. (Tie the strips loosely to allow for air flow.)

slits

TIP:

FOR EXTRA DECORATION, SEW ON FLEECE SHAPES IN CONTRASTING COLORS TO THE OUTSIDE OF YOUR CAGE COVER.

Some pets need time to get used to a new cage or crate cover. Here are some tips to help:

- Place the cover next to the cage or crate for a few days to let your pet get used to it.

- Place the new cover on top of the old one for a few days, removing more and more of the old cover each day.

- Once your pet seems comfortable with the new cover, remove the old one completely.

GLOSSARY

collage (kuh-LAHZH)—a work of art made by gluing pieces of different materials to a flat surface

diameter (dye-AM-uh-tur)—the length of a straight line through the center of a circle

nutritious (noo-TRISH-uhss)—containing elements the body uses to stay strong and healthy

opacity (oh-PA-suh-tee)—the degree to which something allows light through it

parallel (PA-ruh-lel)—an equal distance apart

porous (POR-uhss)—letting liquids pass through

right side—the front side of fabric

seam (SEEM)—a line of sewing that joins two pieces of fabric

wrong side—the back side of fabric

READ MORE

Friday, Megan. *Pet Crafts: Everything You Need to Become Your Pet's Craft Star!* Craft Star. Irvine, Cal.: Walter Foster Pub., 2011.

Ives, Rob. *Amazing Paper Pets: 6 Animated Animals to Make.* New York; London: Sterling Pub. Co., 2010.

Scheunemann, Pam. *Cool Jobs for Young Pet Lovers: Ways to Make Money Caring for Pets.* Cool Kid Jobs. Edina, Minn.: ABDO Pub., 2011.

INTERNET SITES

FactHound offers a safe, fun way to find Internet sites related to this book. All of the sites on FactHound have been researched by our staff.

Here's all you do:

Visit *www.facthound.com*

Type in this code: 9781429676625

Check out projects, games and lots more at
www.capstonekids.com

INDEX